Memories of LOVE

A Treasury of
Childhood Keepsakes

ILLUSTRATED BY
MAREN SCOTT

WORD PUBLISHING
Nashville · London · Vancouver · Melbourne

THIS BOOK TELLS
THE LIFE STORY OF

_____

CONTENTS

YOUR FIRST YEAR
Giggles and Gurgles

The child, the seed, the grain of corn,
The acorn on the hill,
Each for some separate end is born
In season fit, and still
Each must in strength arise to work the
Almighty will.

–Robert Louis Stevenson

Photos

I love the timid things
That gather round the little watercourse
To listen to the frogs with voices hoarse,
And see the squirrels leap and bound at play.
—Laura Ingalls Wilder

GETTING TO KNOW YOU

Your full name is _____

Your name means _____

We gave you this name because _____

_____

Some other names we had in mind were _____

_____

You came to have the nickname _____

Our hopes and dreams for your life. _____

_____

_____

_____

_____

_____

_____

_____

A special blessing for you from your parents. _____

_____

_____

_____

_____

_____

_____

_____

_____

The blessing of the father builds houses for the sons;
the blessing of the mother fills them with good things.

—Rabbi Sirach

GETTING TO KNOW YOUR PARENTS

Mother's full name _____

Mother's date of birth _____

Father's full name _____

Father's date of birth _____

This is how we first met: _____

_____

_____

_____

We were engaged on _____

Your father proposed by _____

_____

_____

_____

We were married on _____

Our marriage took place in _____

Your father wore _____

Your mother wore _____

The person officiating was _____

There is comfort in the strength of love.
—William Wordsworth, "Michael"

Our bridesmaids and groomsmen were _____

_____

_____

Our guests included _____

_____

_____

Some of the things that made our wedding day special were _____

_____

_____

For our honeymoon we went to _____

On our honeymoon we did fun things, like _____

_____

One comical thing that happened on our honeymoon was _____

_____

_____

Let me tell you about our first home. _____

_____

_____

Your mother worked as a _____

Your father worked as a _____

Some of the fun things we did together as newlyweds. _____

_____

_____

_____

_____

_____

Love binds together all the virtues in perfect unity.
—Johann Christoph Arnold

WHILE WAITING FOR YOU

We first knew you were coming when _____

_____

_____

_____

_____

The predicted date of your arrival. _____

Your mother first felt you move on _____

The doctor's name. _____

The first people we told were _____

This is what we did to prepare for your arrival. _____

_____

_____

_____

_____

_____

Before you were born we nicknamed you _____

Your mother craved _____

Your father craved _____

We knew you were scheduled for immediate arrival when _____

_____

_____

_____

_____

_____

Lord, we long for our child,
Borne out of covenant love
Nurtured in love, hope, forgiveness,
Received as gift, blessing, joy.
Barrowby

—"Before Birth. A Waiting Prayer"

A PRAYER FOR YOU, PRECIOUS BABY

Jesus friend of little children,
Be a friend to me
Take my hand and ever keep me
Close to thee.

Teach me how to grow in goodness,
Daily as I grow.
Thou hast been a child, and surely
Thou dost know.

Never leave me, nor forsake me;
Ever be my friend;
For I need thee, from life's dawning
To its very end.

Walter J. Mathams (1853-1931)

You created my inmost being;
you knit me together in my mother's womb.

—Psalm 139:13

YOUR GRAND ENTRANCE

Date. _____

Time. _____

Place. _____

You were _____ inches long.

You weighed _____ pounds _____ ounces.

The color of your hair. _____

The color of your eyes. _____

Your most striking feature. _____

We are sure you inherited this feature from _____

These were the most memorable moments of your birth. _____

_____

_____

_____

_____

_____

Friends who visited were _____

_____

_____

_____

You received these lovely gifts. _____

_____

_____

_____

_____

_____

When a baby comes into the world
it is as though the pure air of heaven
comes along.

—Johann Christoph Arnold

Your favorite lullaby. _____

_____

_____

_____

_____

_____

_____

_____

Sweet dreams form a shade,
O're my lovely infant's head.
Sweet dreams of pleasant streams.
Be happy silent, moony beams.

— William Blake
(from "A Cradle Song")

THIS WAS THE WORLD WHEN YOU WERE BORN

_____ was President.

Some important world events. _____

_____

Important local events. _____

_____

_____

The people making history around the world were _____

_____

_____

What was popular.

Movies. _____

Television programs. _____

Songs. _____

Fashions. _____

Foods. _____

YOUR GODPARENTS (GUARDIANS)

Your godmother's (guardian's) name. _____

Godmother's address. _____

_____

Your godfather's (guardian's) name. _____

Godfather's address. _____

_____

We chose these godparents because _____

_____

_____

They gave you these special gifts. _____

_____

_____

They had this to say about you. _____

_____

_____

_____

photos

The little children are God's life.
There can never be enough of them.

—Mother Teresa

CELEBRATE EACH BLESSED CHILD

Date of dedication. _____

Place. _____

Minister. _____

Guests included _____

_____

Significant events of the day. _____

_____

Date of baptism. _____

Place. _____

Minister (or priest). _____

Guests included _____

_____

Significant events of the day. _____

_____

Date of first communion. _____

Place. _____

Minister (or priest). _____

Significant events of the day. _____

_____

Other religious milestones. _____

_____

_____

_____

_____

_____

And so little Tommy, in a white suit and bare feet,
was christened, quite in order,
with water from the stream at Thornhill,
where the watercress grows.

—Dee Hardie

BABY'S PROUD PROGRESS

Slept through the night _____

Smiled _____

Laughed out loud _____

Gave a kiss _____

Turned over _____

Sat up alone _____

Crawled _____

Drank from a cup _____

Ate solid food _____

Used a spoon _____

Stood alone _____

Took a step _____

Walked alone _____

First word _____

Waved good-bye _____

Got a hair cut _____

Turned a somersault _____

Took a trip _____

A berry ripens in its own good time—
and so does a child's readiness.

—Fred Rogers

HAPPY FIRST BIRTHDAY!

We celebrated by _____

We invited _____

For treats we served _____

Gifts you received. _____

_____

_____

_____

The most memorable moment was _____

_____

_____

You responded to the celebration by _____

_____

_____

Our birthday blessing for you. _____

_____

_____

_____

_____

photos

Nobody can be uncheered by a balloon.

—A. A. Milne, "Winnie-the-Pooh"

YOUR CHILDHOOD HEALTH CHART

Blood type _____

Allergies _____

(date of doctor visit)   (comments)

One month old _____ _____

_____

Two months old _____ _____

_____

Three months old _____ _____

_____

Four months old _____ _____

_____

Five months old _____ _____

_____

YOUR RECORD OF CHILDHOOD ILLNESSES.

Measles _____

German measles _____

Mumps _____

Whooping cough _____

Scarlet fever _____

Flu _____

Other illnesses _____

Surgeries or emergency treatments _____

_____

_____

_____

_____

YOUR RECORD OF CHILDHOOD IMMUNIZATIONS.

	original	booster	booster
DTP	_____	_____	_____
Polio	_____	_____	_____
Measles/mumps /Rubella	_____	_____	_____
Hepatitis B	_____	_____	_____
Chicken pox	_____	_____	_____
Haemophilus B	_____	_____	_____
Others	_____	_____	_____

PRESCHOOL YEARS
Laughing, Playing, & Growing

When I was one
I had just begun.
When I was two,
I was nearly new.
When I was three,
I was hardly me.
When I was four,
I was not much more.

— A. A. Milne

photos

Little lamb, who made thee?
Dost thou know who made thee? . . .
He is meek and he is mild,
He became a little child,
I a child and thou a lamb
We are called by his name.
Little Lamb God bless thee.

—William Blake (1789)

LOOK WHAT YOU CAN DO!

Brush your teeth _____

Wash your hands _____

Use the potty _____

Tie your shoes _____

Zip your zipper _____

Put on your mittens and boots _____

Button your buttons _____

Whistle _____

Count to ten _____

Identify the primary colors _____

Read _____

Say your telephone number _____

Say your address _____

Help with the household chores _____

Others things you learned to do _____

_____

_____

_____

_____

What feeling is so nice as a child's hand in yours?
So small, so soft and warm,
like a kitten huddling in the shelter of your clasp.

—Marjorie Holmes

NOW YOU ARE TWO

We celebrated by _____

_____

We invited _____

_____

For treats we served _____

_____

Gifts you received. _____

_____

_____

You enjoyed the party most when _____

_____

The most memorable moment was _____

_____

_____

You responded to the celebration by _____

_____

Our birthday blessing for you _____

_____

_____

_____

photo

Every eel hopes to become a whale.
—German Proverb

LEARNING ABOUT GOD

You first attended Sunday school at _____

_____

You were _____ years old.

Your teacher's name was _____

Your favorite class activities were _____

_____

_____

The first Bible verse you memorized was _____

_____

_____

Your first prayer. _____

_____

_____

_____

_____

Your favorite song. _____

_____

_____

_____

_____

For family devotions we _____

_____

_____

_____

_____

Little ones to Him belong,
They are weak but He is strong.

−hymn, "Jesus Loves Me"

23

CAN IT BE? YOU ARE THREE!

We celebrated by _____

_____

We invited _____

_____

For treats we served _____

_____

Gifts you received. _____

_____

_____

_____

You enjoyed the party most when _____

_____

The most memorable moment was _____

_____

_____

_____

Our birthday blessing for you. _____

_____

_____

photo

A lap is so you don't get crumbs on the floor.

Ruth Krauss, "A Hole Is to Dig"

SEE, THIS IS ME!

You attended preschool at _____
_____

Your teacher's name. _____

Your best friends. _____
_____

Your favorite activities at preschool. _____
_____
_____

At home you helped with family chores by _____
_____
_____
_____

We will never forget when you _____
_____
_____
_____
_____

We laughed and laughed when you _____
_____
_____
_____
_____

You said the cutest things! _____
_____
_____
_____
_____
_____

Sometimes a cheering surprise just happens along.

—A. A. Milne, "Winnie-the-Pooh"

BIRTHDAY NUMBER FOUR

We celebrated by _____

_____

We invited _____

_____

For treats we served _____

_____

You enjoyed the party most when _____

_____

_____

Gifts you received. _____

_____

_____

The most memorable moment was _____

_____

_____

You responded to the celebration by _____

_____

Our birthday blessing for you. _____

_____

_____

photo

If there's anything half so much fun as being alive,
I'd like to know what it is!

−Mary Engelbreit

THESE WERE YOUR FAVORITES WHEN YOU WERE FOUR

song _____

book _____

story _____

indoor game _____

outdoor game _____

secret hiding place _____

toy _____

friend _____

animal _____

color _____

pet _____

Bible character _____

Bible story _____

Bible verse _____

place to play _____

snack _____

fast food _____

flavor of ice cream _____

I am not afraid of storms
for I am learning how
to sail my ship.

–Louisa May Alcott

YOUR PERSONALITY AT FOUR

If you had a boat what would you name it? _____

Why would you name it that? _____

_____

If you could be any animal, what would you like to be? _____

Why that animal? _____

_____

If you could have any present, what would you like to have? _____

Why that present? _____

_____

What would you like to be when you grow up? _____

Why does that interest you? _____

_____

What things scare you most? _____

Why do they scare you? _____

_____

Draw a picture of your house.

A sense of individual identity is one of the greatest gifts that parents can give a child.

Fred Rogers

KINDERGARTEN & ELEMENTARY

Running, Jumping, and Learning

When the voices of children are
heard on the green
And laughing is heard on the hill,
My heart is at rest within my breast
And everything else is still.

—William Blake, "Nurse's Song"

photos

Let us celebrate each child as best, most adored,
most surely blessed.

—Walter Dean Myers, "Glorious Angels"

'SAKES ALIVE! YOU ARE FIVE!

We celebrated by _____

_____

We invited _____

_____

For treats we served _____

Gifts you received. _____

_____

_____

_____

You enjoyed the party most when _____

_____

The most memorable moment was _____

_____

Our birthday blessing for you. _____

_____

_____

_____

_____

_____

photos

Picturing a special future is one way
of planting hope deep in a child's heart.

—Gary Smalley and John Trent

OFF TO SCHOOL

This is what we did to get ready for your first day of school . _____
_____
_____

Your first day in school was _____

You went to school at _____

Your teacher's name. _____

Your reaction to this new adventure. _____
_____

Our reaction was _____
_____

Your comments about school. _____
_____

What you liked about school. _____
_____

What you definitely did **not** like. _____
_____

Your drawing of school.

This is how you write your name._____

"What does Christopher Robin do in the morning?
He learns. He becomes Educated."

—A. A. Milne, "The House at Pooh Corner"

YOU ARE FIVE AND GROWING

This year you learned how to _____

_____

_____

Your new interests and activities included _____

_____

_____

The things you enjoy doing most. _____

_____

_____

Your best friends. _____

_____

Your chores. _____

_____

_____

We were so proud of you when _____

_____

_____

You made us laugh when _____

_____

_____

Unforgettable things you said. _____

_____

_____

_____

Books we read to you this year._____

_____

There is no frigate like a book to take us lands away.

—Emily Dickinson

FAMILY COMINGS AND GOINGS IN _____
(year)

Significant family news events. _____

_____

_____

World news events. _____

_____

_____

Intriguing guests we had in our home. _____

_____

_____

To help others in our community we _____

_____

_____

Struggles our family overcame. _____

_____

_____

Things that brought us special happiness. _____

_____

_____

The most fun thing we did was _____

_____

_____

The most interesting places we visited were _____

_____

_____

Where money is not so important as loving-kindness.
Where even the teakettle sings from happiness.
That is home. God bless it.

—Madame Ernestine Schumann-Heink

34

TURNING SUNNY, FUNNY SIX

We celebrated by _____
_____

We invited _____
_____

For treats we served _____
_____

Gifts you received. _____
_____
_____

You enjoyed the celebration most when _____
_____

The most memorable moment was _____
_____

Our birthday blessing for you. _____
_____
_____
_____
_____

photos

It is the inalienable right of a child
to have something of his very own.

−Laura Ingalls Wilder

SO MUCH FUN IN GRADE ONE

Name and address of school. _____

_____

The name of your teacher. _____

Your favorite school subject. _____

Your most challenging subject. _____

Your best friend. _____

Your favorite recess activity. _____

Your favorite food for lunch. _____

After-school activities included _____

We attended your open house on _____

Our observations. _____

_____

_____

_____

_____

Competitions entered and awards won. _____

_____

_____

Special school projects. _____

_____

School activities and class trips. _____

_____

_____

Your height _____

Your weight _____

The events of childhood do not pass,
but repeat themselves like seasons of the year.

—Eleanor Farjeon

This is how you write your name _____

The best thing that happened to you this year was _____

_____

_____

The worst thing that happened to you this year was _____

_____

_____

The funniest thing that happened to you this year was _____

_____

_____

What we did on Thanksgiving. _____

_____

What we did at Christmas. _____

_____

What we did during the summer. _____

_____

Books you read this year. _____

_____

_____

This year you learned how to _____

_____

_____

Your chores included _____

_____

_____

Mud is to jump in and slide in and yell doodleedoodeleedoo.

—Ruth Krauss, "A Hole Is to Dig"

GOD BE IN MY HEART

We attended church at _____

_____

Our pastor (priest) was _____

Your Sunday school teacher was _____

_____

Special class activities you enjoyed. _____

_____

Church programs you participated in. _____

_____

_____

Your favorite chorus or hymn was _____

_____

For family devotions this year we _____

_____

_____

Significant prayer requests this year included _____

_____

_____

_____

God answered our prayers by _____

_____

_____

_____

A spiritual milestone in your life this year was _____

_____

_____

Lord Jesus Christ, be with me today
And help me in all I think, and do, and say.

−Traditional Prayer

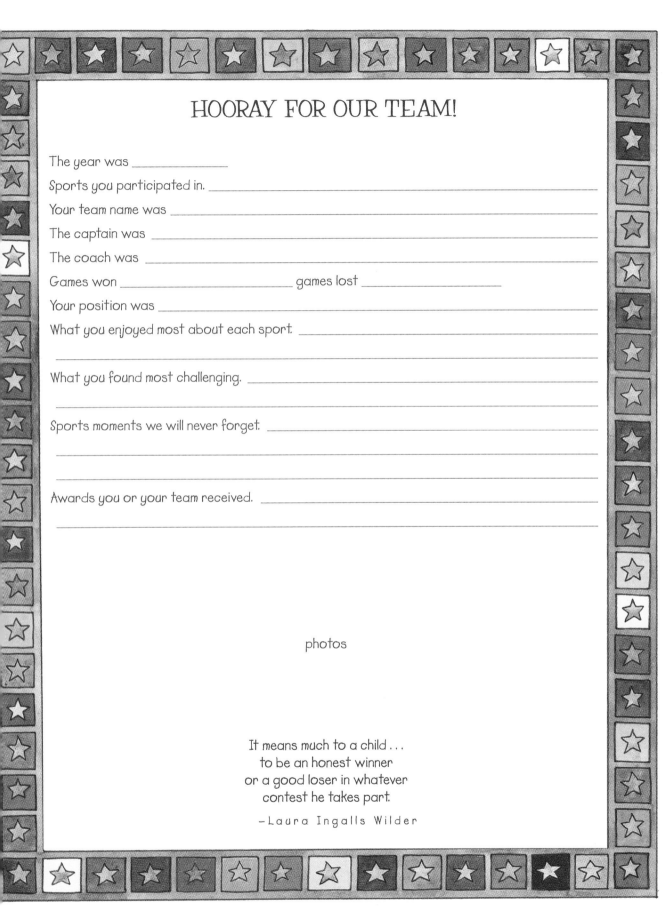

HOORAY FOR OUR TEAM!

The year was _____

Sports you participated in. _____

Your team name was _____

The captain was _____

The coach was _____

Games won _____ games lost _____

Your position was _____

What you enjoyed most about each sport. _____

_____

What you found most challenging. _____

_____

Sports moments we will never forget. _____

_____

_____

Awards you or your team received. _____

_____

photos

It means much to a child . . .
to be an honest winner
or a good loser in whatever
contest he takes part.

−Laura Ingalls Wilder

LONG WALKS IN THE WOODS

To develop an appreciation of nature we _____
_____
_____

Some of the parks, natural wonders, or scientific exhibits we visited. _____
_____
_____

You were most fascinated by _____
_____
_____

To develop an interest in gardens and plants we _____
_____
_____

We helped to keep the environment clean by _____
_____
_____

Animals and pets you cared for. _____
_____
_____

You took care of them by _____
_____
_____

"If I plant a honeycomb outside my house,
then it will grow up into a beehive."

−Pooh in "The House at Pooh Corner"

WATER-COLORED MEMORIES

To develop an appreciation of the arts we _____
_____
_____

Museums, art galleries, or cultural events we visited. _____
_____

You were most impressed by _____
_____

What you found most intriguing there. _____
_____
_____

To encourage your musical abilities we _____
_____
_____

Musical instruments you studied. _____
_____

Your music teacher. _____
Your favorite pieces of music. _____
_____

Perhaps the thing that the arts do best is open doors to learning.
—Charles Fowler

FAMILY COMINGS AND GOINGS IN _____

(year)

Significant family news events. _____
_____
_____

World news events. _____
_____
_____

Intriguing guests we had in our home. _____
_____
_____

To help others in our community we _____
_____
_____

Struggles our family overcame. _____
_____

Things that brought us special happiness. _____
_____
_____

The most fun thing we did was _____
_____
_____

The most interesting places we visited were _____
_____
_____

If we really want peace in the world,
let us first love one another in the family.
—Mother Teresa

NOW YOU ARE SILLY SEVEN!

We celebrated by _____

_____

We invited _____

_____

For treats we served _____

_____

Gifts you received. _____

_____

_____

You enjoyed the party most when _____

_____

The most memorable moment was _____

_____

Our birthday blessing for you. _____

_____

_____

_____

photos

Childhood is a carefree time when best friends
are made, promises are kept,
and there is always time to dream.

−Mary Engelbreit

13

UNIQUELY YOU IN GRADE TWO

Name and address of school. _____

_____

The name of your teacher. _____

Your favorite school subject.. _____

Your most challenging subject. _____

Your best friend. _____

Favorite recess activities included _____

Your favorite food for lunch. _____

After-school activities included _____

We attended your open house on _____

Our observations. _____

_____

Competitions entered and awards won. _____

_____

_____

Special school projects. _____

_____

School activities and class trips. _____

_____

Your height _____

Your weight _____

We wove a web in childhood,
a web of sunny air.

—Charlotte Brontë

Your favorite color is _____

The best thing that happened to you this year was _____
_____
_____

The worst thing that happened to you this year was _____
_____
_____

The funniest thing that happened to you this year was _____
_____
_____

What we did on Thanksgiving. _____
_____

What we did at Christmas. _____
_____

What we did during the summer. _____
_____

Books you read this year. _____
_____
_____
_____

This year you learned how to _____
_____
_____

Your chores were _____
_____

He shall gather the lambs with his arm,
and carry them in his bosom.

−Isaiah 40.11

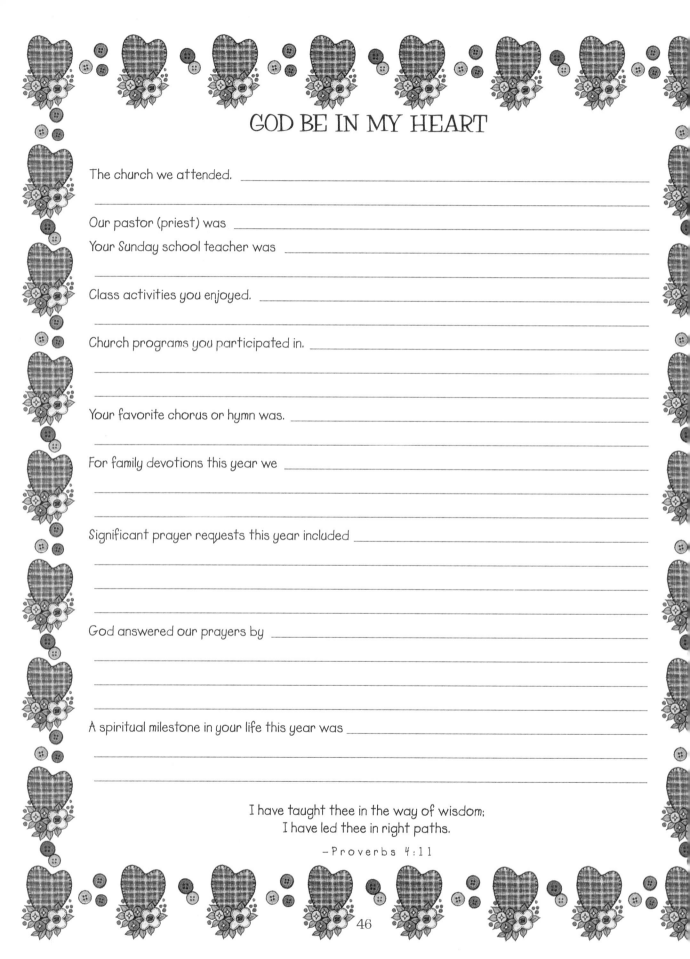

GOD BE IN MY HEART

The church we attended. _____

_____

Our pastor (priest) was _____

Your Sunday school teacher was _____

_____

Class activities you enjoyed. _____

_____

Church programs you participated in. _____

_____

_____

Your favorite chorus or hymn was. _____

_____

For family devotions this year we _____

_____

_____

Significant prayer requests this year included _____

_____

_____

_____

God answered our prayers by _____

_____

_____

_____

A spiritual milestone in your life this year was _____

_____

_____

I have taught thee in the way of wisdom;
I have led thee in right paths.

−Proverbs 4:11

HOORAY FOR OUR TEAM!

The year was _____

Sports you participated in. _____

Your team name was _____

The captain was _____

The coach was _____

Games won _____ games lost _____

Your position was _____

What you enjoyed most about each sport. _____

_____

What you found most challenging. _____

_____

Sports moments we will never forget. _____

_____

_____

Awards you or your team received. _____

_____

photos

Whatever you can do, or dream you can, begin it.
— J. W. von Goethe

LONG WALKS IN THE WOODS

To develop an appreciation of nature we _____

_____

Some of the parks, natural wonders, or scientific exhibits we visited. _____

_____

You were most fascinated by _____

_____

To develop an interest in gardens and plants we _____

_____

We helped to keep the environment clean by _____

_____

Animals and pets you cared for. _____

_____

You took care of them by _____

_____

All the little streams higher up in the Forest
went this way and that . . . having so much
to find out before it was too late.

—A. A. Milne, The House at Pooh Corner

WATER-COLORED MEMORIES

To develop an appreciation of the arts we _____
_____
_____

Museums, art galleries, or cultural events we visited. _____
_____

You were most impressed by _____
_____

What you found most intriguing there. _____
_____

To encourage your musical abilities we _____
_____
_____

Musical instruments you studied _____
_____

Your music teacher. _____
_____

Your favorite pieces of music. _____
_____

Every bird loves to hear himself sing.

—German Proverb

FAMILY COMINGS AND GOINGS IN ________

(year)

Significant family news events. ____________________

____

____

World news events. ____________________

____

____

Intriguing guests we had in our home. ____________________

____

____

To help others in our community we ____________________

____

____

Struggles our family overcame. ____________________

____

____

Things that brought us special happiness. ____________________

____

____

The most fun thing we did was ____________________

____

____

The most interesting places we visited were ____________________

____

____

No matter where life takes us, we cherish the good times.

—Emyl Jenkins

ISN'T IT GREAT? YOU ARE EIGHT!

We celebrated by _____

_____

We invited _____

_____

For treats we served _____

_____

Gifts you received. _____

_____

_____

You enjoyed the party most when _____

_____

The most memorable moment was _____

_____

Our birthday blessing for you. _____

_____

_____

_____

_____

photos

It is not how much we have,
but how much we enjoy it,
that makes for happiness.

—Anonymous

ALL YOU CAN BE IN GRADE THREE

Name and address of school _____

_____

The name of your teacher. _____

Your favorite school subject. _____

Your most challenging subject. _____

Your best friend. _____

Favorite recess activities included _____

Your favorite food for lunch. _____

After-school activities included _____

We attended your open house on _____

Our observations. _____

_____

Competitions entered and awards won. _____

_____

_____

_____

Special school projects. _____

_____

School activities and class trips. _____

_____

Your height _____

Your weight _____

Children of all ages need the daily
"food and clothing" of love and acceptance.

− G a r y S m a l l e y a n d J o h n T r e n t

When you grow up you want to be _____

The best thing that happened to you this year was _____

_____

_____

The worst thing that happened to you this year was _____

_____

_____

The funniest thing that happened to you this year was _____

_____

_____

What we did on Thanksgiving. _____

_____

What we did at Christmas. _____

_____

What we did during the summer. _____

_____

Books you read this year. _____

_____

_____

_____

This year you learned how to _____

_____

_____

Your chores were _____

_____

_____

Backward, turn backward,
O time, in your flight,
Make me a child again
just for tonight.

—Elizabeth Akers Allen

GOD BE IN MY HEART

The church we attended. _____
_____

Our pastor (priest) was _____

Your Sunday school teacher was _____
_____

Class activities you enjoyed. _____
_____

Church programs you participated in. _____
_____
_____

Your favorite chorus or hymn. _____
_____

For family devotions this year we _____
_____
_____

Significant prayer requests this year included _____
_____
_____

God answered our prayers by _____
_____
_____

A spiritual milestone in your life this year was _____
_____
_____
_____

To a child, the world of God and his angels is
often much closer and more real than we suspect.

—Johann Christoph Arnold

HOORAY FOR OUR TEAM!

The year was _____

Sports you participated in. _____

Your team name was _____

The captain was _____

The coach was _____

Games won _____ games lost _____

Your position was _____

What you enjoyed most about the sport. _____
_____

What you found most challenging. _____
_____

Sports moments we will never forget. _____
_____
_____

Awards you or your team received. _____
_____

photos

No one ever achieved anything
from the smallest to the greatest
unless the dream was dreamed first.

—Laura Ingalls Wilder

LONG WALKS IN THE WOODS

To develop an appreciation of nature we _____
_____
_____

Some of the parks, natural wonders, or scientific exhibits we visited. _____
_____
_____

You were most fascinated by _____
_____
_____

To develop an interest in gardens and plants we _____
_____
_____

We helped to keep the environment clean by _____
_____
_____

Animals and pets you cared for. _____
_____
_____

You took care of them by _____
_____
_____

Keep your face to the sunshine
and you cannot see the shadows.

—Helen Keller

WATER-COLORED MEMORIES

To develop an appreciation of the arts we _____
_____
_____

Museums, art galleries, or cultural events we visited. _____
_____
_____

You were most impressed by _____
_____

What you found most intriguing there. _____
_____

To encourage your musical abilities we _____
_____
_____

Musical instruments you studied. _____
_____

Your music teacher. _____
_____

Your favorite pieces of music. _____
_____

What will a child learn sooner than a song?

—Alexander Pope

FAMILY COMINGS AND GOINGS IN _____

(year)

Significant family news events. _____
_____
_____

World news events. _____
_____
_____

Intriguing guests we had in our home. _____
_____
_____

To help others in our community we _____
_____
_____

Struggles our family overcame. _____
_____
_____

Things that brought us special happiness. _____
_____

The most fun thing we did was _____
_____

The most interesting places we visited were _____
_____
_____

We can do no great things,
only small things with great love.

—Mother Teresa

THESE WERE YOUR FAVORITES WHEN YOU WERE EIGHT

Song _____

Book _____

Saying _____

Indoor game _____

Outdoor game _____

Sport _____

Secret hideaway _____

Toy _____

Friend _____

Animal _____

Color _____

Pet _____

Bible character _____

Bible story _____

Bible verse _____

Place to vacation _____

Snack _____

Fast food _____

Flavor of ice cream _____

"He would be a pirate! That was it!
Now his future lay plain before him,
and glowing with unimaginable splendor."

—Mark Twain, The Adventures of Tom Sawyer

photos

Little deeds of kindness
Little words of love,
Make our earth an Eden,
Like the heavens above.

Julia A. Carney (1823-1908)
and Percy Dearmer (1867-1936)

60

IT'S SUBLIME! YOU'RE TURNING NINE!

We celebrated by _____

_____

We invited _____

_____

For treats we served _____

_____

_____

Gifts you received. _____

_____

_____

You enjoyed the party most when _____

_____

The most memorable moment was _____

_____

Our birthday blessing for you. _____

_____

_____

_____

photos

*Childhood cannot be used over again
for a different set of memories.*

—Edith Schaeffer

LEARNING MUCH MORE IN GRADE FOUR

Name and address of school. _____

_____

Name of teacher. _____

_____

Your favorite school subject.. _____

_____

Your most challenging subject. _____

Your best friend. _____

Favorite recess activities include _____

Your favorite food for lunch. _____

After-school activities included _____

We attended your open house on _____

Our observations. _____

_____

Competitions entered and awards won. _____

_____

_____

_____

Special school projects. _____

_____

School activities and class trips. _____

_____

Your height _____

Your weight _____

A love of learning has a lot to do
with learning that we're loved.

—Fred Rogers

What would you name your very own island? _____

The best thing that happened to you this year was _____

_____

_____

The worst thing that happened to you this year was _____

_____

_____

The funniest thing that happened to you this year was _____

_____

_____

What we did on Thanksgiving. _____

_____

What we did at Christmas. _____

_____

What we did during the summer. _____

_____

Books you read this year. _____

_____

_____

_____

This year you learned how to _____

_____

Your chores were _____

_____

_____

Hear, ye children, the instruction of a father,
and attend to know understanding.

—Proverbs 4.1

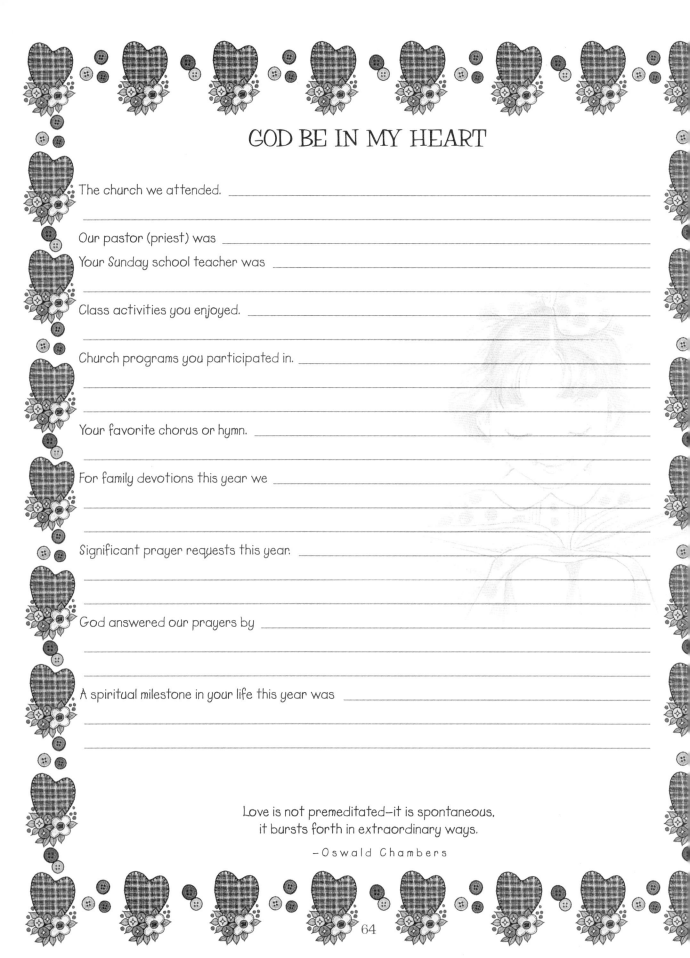

GOD BE IN MY HEART

The church we attended. _____
_____

Our pastor (priest) was _____

Your Sunday school teacher was _____
_____

Class activities you enjoyed. _____
_____

Church programs you participated in. _____
_____
_____

Your favorite chorus or hymn. _____
_____

For family devotions this year we _____
_____
_____

Significant prayer requests this year. _____
_____
_____

God answered our prayers by _____
_____
_____

A spiritual milestone in your life this year was _____
_____
_____

Love is not premeditated—it is spontaneous,
it bursts forth in extraordinary ways.

—Oswald Chambers

HOORAY FOR OUR TEAM!

The year was _____

Sports you participated in. _____

Your team name was _____

The captain was _____

The coach was _____

Games won _____ games lost _____

Your position was _____

What you enjoyed most about the sport. _____
_____

What you found most challenging. _____
_____

Sports moments we will never forget. _____
_____
_____

Awards you or your team received. _____
_____

photos

The young are the builders of tomorrow.

—Mother Teresa

LONG WALKS IN THE WOODS

To develop an appreciation of nature we _____
_____
_____

Some of the parks, natural wonders, or scientific exhibits we visited. _____
_____
_____

You were most fascinated by _____
_____

To develop an interest in gardens and plants we _____
_____
_____
_____

We helped to keep the environment clean by _____
_____

Animals and pets you cared for. _____
_____

You took care of them by _____
_____

A good laugh heals a lot of hurts.

–Madeleine L'Engle

WATER-COLORED MEMORIES

To develop an appreciation of the arts we _____
_____
_____

Museums, art galleries, or cultural events we visited. _____
_____

You were most impressed by _____
_____

What you found most intriguing there. _____
_____

To encourage your musical abilities we _____
_____
_____

Musical instruments you studied. _____
_____

Your music teacher. _____
_____

Your favorite pieces of music. _____
_____

Music, when soft voices die, vibrates in the memory.

—Percy Bysshe Shelley

FAMILY COMINGS AND GOINGS IN _____

(year)

Significant family news events. _____
_____
_____

World news events. _____
_____
_____

Intriguing guests we had in our home. _____
_____
_____

To help others in our community we _____
_____
_____

Struggles our family overcame. _____
_____
_____

Things that brought us special happiness. _____
_____
_____

The most fun thing we did was _____
_____
_____

The most interesting places we visited were _____
_____
_____

Lessons learned at mother's knee last through life.

—Laura Ingalls Wilder

TURNING TERRIFIC TEN!

We celebrated by _____
_____

We invited _____
_____

For treats we served _____
_____

Gifts you received included _____
_____
_____

You enjoyed the party most when _____
_____

The most memorable moment was _____
_____

Our birthday blessing for you. _____
_____
_____
_____

photos

Our words can promote growth by wrapping
others in a cocoon of love and hope.

—Gary Smalley and John Trent

ADVENTURES ALIVE IN GRADE FIVE!

Name and address of school. _____

_____

The name of your teacher. _____

Your favorite school subject. _____

Your most challenging subject. _____

Your best friend. _____

Favorite recess activities included _____

Favorite food for lunch. _____

After-school activities included _____

We attended your open house on _____

Our observations. _____

_____

Competitions entered and awards won. _____

_____

_____

_____

Special school projects. _____

_____

School activities and class trips. _____

_____

Your height _____

Your weight _____

Hear, O my son, and receive my sayings;
and the years of thy life shall be many.

−Proverbs 4.10

What famous person would you like to talk to? _____

The best thing that happened to you this year was _____

_____

_____

The worst thing that happened to you this year was _____

_____

_____

The funniest thing that happened to you this year was _____

_____

_____

What we did on Thanksgiving. _____

_____

What we did at Christmas. _____

_____

What we did during the summer. _____

_____

Books you read this year. _____

_____

This year you learned how to _____

_____

_____

Your chores were _____

_____

_____

The one who misses all the fun
Is he who says, "It can't be done."

—William J. Bennett

GOD BE IN MY HEART

The church we attended. _____
_____

Our pastor (priest) was _____

Your Sunday school teacher was _____
_____

Class activities you enjoyed. _____
_____

Church programs you participated in. _____
_____
_____

Your favorite chorus or hymn. _____
_____

For family devotions this year we _____
_____
_____

Significant prayer requests this year. _____
_____
_____

God answered our prayers by _____
_____
_____
_____

A spiritual milestone in your life this year was _____
_____
_____

O God, make us children of quietness, and heirs of peace.

—St. Clement

72

HOORAY FOR OUR TEAM!

The year was _____

Sports you participated in. _____

Your team name was _____

The captain was _____

The coach was _____

Games won _____ games lost _____

Your position was _____

What you enjoyed most about each sport. _____

_____

What you found most challenging. _____

_____

Sports moments we will never forget. _____

_____

_____

Awards you or your team received. _____

_____

photos

In helping others to happiness
we are on the road
to the same goal ourselves.

–Richard Cardinal Cushing

LONG WALKS IN THE WOODS

To develop an appreciation of nature we _____

_____

_____

Some of the parks, natural wonders, or scientific exhibits we visited. _____

_____

_____

Your were most fascinated by _____

_____

_____

To develop an interest in gardens and plants we _____

_____

_____

_____

We helped to keep the environment clean by _____

_____

Animals and pets you cared for. _____

_____

You took care of them by _____

_____

The Sun does arise,
and make happy the skies.

—William Blake, "The Echoing Green"

WATER-COLORED MEMORIES

To develop an appreciation of the arts we _____
_____
_____

Museums, art galleries, or cultural events we visited. _____
_____

You were most impressed by _____
_____

What you found most intriguing there. _____
_____

To encourage your musical abilities we _____
_____
_____

Musical instruments you studied. _____
_____

Your music teacher. _____
_____

Your favorite pieces of music. _____
_____

Poetry and Hums aren't things which you get, they're things which get you.
And all you can do is to go where they can find you.

—A. A. Milne, "The House at Pooh Corner"

FAMILY COMINGS AND GOINGS IN _____

(year)

Significant family news events. _____

_____

_____

World news events. _____

_____

_____

Intriguing guests we had in our home. _____

_____

_____

To help others in our community we. _____

_____

_____

Struggles our family overcame. _____

_____

_____

Things that brought us special happiness. _____

_____

_____

The most fun thing we did was _____

_____

_____

The most interesting places we visited were _____

_____

_____

Home is where one starts from.

-T. S. Eliot

WHAT FUN—TO BE ELEVEN!

We celebrated by _____

_____

We invited _____

_____

For treats we served _____

_____

Gifts you received _____

_____

_____

You enjoyed the party most when _____

_____

The most memorable event was _____

_____

Our birthday blessing for you. _____

_____

_____

_____

photos

Let us celebrate the children.
Let us spin mysteries for their minds
and wonders for their hearts.

—Walter Dean Myers, "Glorious Angels"

SCORING HIGH IN GRADE SIX

Name and address of school. _____

_____

The name of your teacher. _____

Your favorite school subject. _____

You most challenging subject. _____

Your best friend. _____

Favorite recess activities included _____

Your favorite food for lunch. _____

After-school activities included _____

We attended your open house on _____

Our observations. _____

_____

Competitions entered and awards won. _____

_____

_____

Special school projects. _____

_____

School activities and class trips. _____

_____

Your height _____

Your weight _____

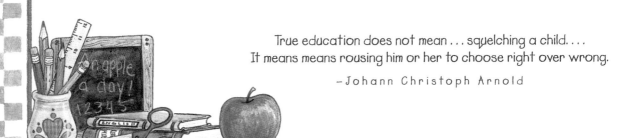

True education does not mean . . . squelching a child. . . .
It means means rousing him or her to choose right over wrong.

– Johann Christoph Arnold

78

This is how you write your name _____

The best thing that happened to you this year was _____
_____
_____

The worst thing that happened to you this year was _____
_____
_____

The funniest thing that happened to you this year was _____
_____
_____

What we did on Thanksgiving. _____
_____

What we did at Christmas. _____
_____

What we did during the summer. _____
_____

Books you read this year. _____
_____
_____
_____

This year you learned how to _____
_____
_____

Your chores were _____
_____
_____

Our hopes for tomorrow are rooted in the past.

–Emyl Jenkins

GOD BE IN MY HEART

The church we attended. _____
_____

Our pastor (priest) was _____
_____

Your Sunday school teacher was _____
_____

Class activities you enjoyed. _____
_____

Church programs you participated in. _____
_____
_____

Your favorite chorus or hymn. _____
_____

For family devotions this year we _____
_____
_____

Significant prayer requests this year. _____
_____
_____

God answered our prayers by _____
_____
_____

A spiritual milestone in your life this year was _____
_____
_____

To a child, the world of God and his angels
is often much closer and more real than we suspect.

–Johann Christoph Arnold

HOORAY FOR OUR TEAM!

The year was _____

Sports you participated in. _____

Your team name was _____

The captain was _____

The coach was _____

Games won _____ games lost _____

Your position was _____

What you enjoyed most about each sport. _____
_____

What you found most challenging. _____
_____

Sports moments we will never forget. _____
_____
_____

Awards you or your team received. _____
_____

photos

If you're really determined, you must go forward.
Keep going forward, and mind you take the right road.

—"The Stars in the Sky"

LONG WALKS IN THE WOODS

To develop an appreciation of nature we _____
_____
_____

Some of the parks, natural wonders, or scientific exhibits we visited. _____
_____
_____

You were most fascinated by _____
_____

To develop an interest in gardens and plants we _____
_____
_____
_____

We helped to keep the environment clean by _____
_____

Animals and pets you cared for. _____
_____

You took care of them by _____
_____

In every child there is a love for the earth,
a joy in the starry sky,
and a warm fondness for everything living.

–Johann Christoph Arnold

WATER-COLORED MEMORIES

To develop an appreciation of the arts we _____

_____

_____

Museums, art galleries, or cultural events we visited. _____

_____

You were most impressed by _____

_____

What you found most intriguing there. _____

_____

To encourage your musical abilities we _____

_____

_____

Musical instruments you studied. _____

_____

Your music teacher. _____

_____

Your favorite pieces of music. _____

_____

Fortunately for children, the uncertainties of the present
always give way to the enchanted possibilities of the future.

—Gelsey Kirkland

FAMILY COMINGS AND GOINGS IN _____

(year)

Significant family news events. _____

_____

_____

World news events. _____

_____

_____

Intriguing guests we had in our home. _____

_____

_____

To help others in our community we _____

_____

_____

Struggles our family overcame. _____

_____

_____

Things that brought us special happiness. _____

_____

_____

The most fun thing we did was _____

_____

_____

The most interesting places we visited were _____

_____

_____

Manners are a sensitive awareness of the feelings of others.

−Emily Post

TODAY YOU ARE TWELVE

You wanted to celebrate by _____

_____

Friends you invited. _____

_____

Activities we planned. _____

_____

_____

Foods we served. _____

_____

Gifts you received _____

_____

_____

The most memorable moment was _____

_____

The funniest moment was _____

_____

_____

Our birthday blessing for you. _____

_____

_____

_____

_____

photos

Fond memory brings the light of other days around me.
– Thomas More

SHAPING YOUR FUTURE IN GRADE SEVEN

Name and address of school. _____

_____

Your favorite school subject. _____

_____

Your favorite teacher. _____

Your most challenging subject. _____

Your best friend. _____

Your favorite food for lunch. _____

After school you like to _____

_____

We attended your open house on _____

Our observations. _____

_____

School competitions entered and awards won. _____

_____

Special school projects. _____

_____

School activities and class trips. _____

_____

The part of the school day you look forward to most. _____

_____

Not everything is said in words;
sometimes you have to listen
between the lines.

—Charles Blaine Adams

Your favorite expression. _____

The best thing that happened to you this year was _____
_____
_____

The worst thing that happened to you this year was _____
_____
_____

The funniest thing that happened to you this year was _____
_____
_____

What we did on Thanksgiving. _____
_____

What we did at Christmas. _____
_____

What you did during the summer. _____
_____
_____

Books you read this year. _____
_____
_____
_____

This year you learned how to _____
_____

Your chores were _____
_____
_____

Books are the quietest and most constant of friends.

–Charles W. Eliot

SCORE ONE FOR OUR TEAM

The year was _____

Sports you participated in. _____
_____

Your team name was _____

The captain was _____

The coach was _____

Games won _____ games lost _____

Your position was _____

What you enjoyed most about each sport. _____
_____

What you found most challenging. _____
_____

Sports moments we will never forget. _____
_____
_____

Awards you or your team received. _____
_____

photos

The highest reward for man's toil
is not what he gets for it
but what he becomes by it.

—John Ruskin

BE ALL YOU CAN BE

Extracurricular activities and lessons you participated in. _____

_____

Where and when you were involved. _____

_____

Who was the instructor(s)? _____

_____

What fascinated you most about each? _____

_____

Things you did to improve your knowledge and skills in each activity. _____

_____

_____

_____

To encourage your development in these skills we _____

_____

_____

_____

Which activity brought you the most satisfaction? _____

_____

Awards, honors, and special recognition for each activity. _____

_____

_____

_____

I have rarely been free from the disturbing realization
that my playing might have been better.

−Ignacy Jan Paderewski

GOD BE IN MY HEART

The church we attended. _____
_____

Our pastor (priest) was _____
_____

Your Sunday school teacher was _____
_____

Special friends you enjoyed. _____
_____

Church programs you participated in. _____
_____
_____

Your favorite chorus or hymn. _____
_____

For family devotions this year we _____
_____
_____

Significant prayer requests this year. _____
_____
_____

God answered our prayers by _____
_____
_____

A spiritual milestone in your life this year was _____
_____
_____

Heaven is not reached at a single bound;
. . . We mount to its summit round by round.

—Josiah Gilbert Holland

Personal goals we helped you set for the year _____

    1. _____

    2. _____

    3. _____

    4. _____

This is how you want to grow personally. _____

_____

_____

This is how you want to grow spiritually. _____

_____

_____

This is how you want to improve your relationships with others.

_____

_____

These are the plans you made to reach your goals.

    1. _____

    2. _____

    3. _____

These are the steps you took to reach your goals.

    1. _____

    2. _____

    3. _____

The progress you made toward each of your goals for this year.

    1. _____

    2. _____

    3. _____

    4. _____

What you are is God's gift to you, What you make of yourself is your gift to God.

—Anonymous

FAMILY COMINGS AND GOINGS IN ＿＿＿＿＿

(year)

Significant family news events. ＿＿＿＿＿＿＿＿＿＿＿＿＿＿＿＿＿＿＿＿＿＿＿＿＿
＿＿＿
＿＿＿

World news events. ＿＿＿＿＿＿＿＿＿＿＿＿＿＿＿＿＿＿＿＿＿＿＿＿＿＿＿＿＿＿＿＿＿
＿＿＿
＿＿＿

Intriguing guests we had in our home. ＿＿＿＿＿＿＿＿＿＿＿＿＿＿＿＿＿＿＿＿＿＿＿
＿＿＿
＿＿＿

To help others in our community we ＿＿＿＿＿＿＿＿＿＿＿＿＿＿＿＿＿＿＿＿＿＿＿＿
＿＿＿
＿＿＿

Struggles our family overcame. ＿＿＿＿＿＿＿＿＿＿＿＿＿＿＿＿＿＿＿＿＿＿＿＿＿＿
＿＿＿
＿＿＿

Things that brought us special happiness. ＿＿＿＿＿＿＿＿＿＿＿＿＿＿＿＿＿＿＿＿
＿＿＿
＿＿＿

The most fun thing we did was ＿＿＿＿＿＿＿＿＿＿＿＿＿＿＿＿＿＿＿＿＿＿＿＿＿＿＿
＿＿＿
＿＿＿

The most interesting places we visited were ＿＿＿＿＿＿＿＿＿＿＿＿＿＿＿＿＿＿＿
＿＿＿
＿＿＿

Whoso loves believes the impossible.
—Elizabeth Barrett Browning

YOUR PERSONALITY AT TWELVE

If you ruled a make-believe kingdom what would you name it? _____
_____

Why would you name it that? _____

_____

If you could be any animal, what would you like to be? _____
Why that animal? _____

_____

What would be the most wonderful present you could receive? _____

_____

Why would that be so wonderful? _____

_____

What would you like to be when you grow up? _____
Why? _____

_____

What two things are you most afraid of? _____
Why are you afraid of them? _____

_____

If you could travel anywhere in the world for two weeks where would you like to go? _____

_____

What would you like to do there? _____

_____

What do you feel the most confident doing? _____
_____

What do you feel the least confident doing? _____

_____

What is your favorite color? _____
What is your favorite candy bar? _____

There is always one moment in childhood
when the door opens and lets in the future.

–Graham Greene

photos

It's you I like,
It's not the things you wear,
It's not the way you do your hair,
But it's **you** I like.

—Fred Rogers,
"It's You I Like"

IT'S TERRIFIC TO BE THIRTEEN

You wanted to celebrate by _____
_____

Friends you invited. _____
_____

Activities we planned. _____
_____
_____

Foods we served. _____
_____

Gifts you received _____
_____
_____

The most memorable moment was _____
_____

The funniest moment was _____
_____
_____

Our birthday blessing for you. _____
_____
_____

photos

Make the most of yourself . . . for that is all there is of you.
—Ralph Waldo Emerson

GO FOR THE GOLD IN GRADE EIGHT

Name and address of school. _____

_____

Your favorite school subject. _____

Your favorite teacher. _____

Your most challenging subject. _____

Your best friend. _____

Your favorite food for lunch. _____

After school you like to _____

_____

We attended your open house on _____

_____

Our observations. _____

_____

School competitions entered and awards won. _____

_____

_____

Special school projects. _____

_____

School activities and class trips. _____

_____

The part of the school day you look forward to most. _____

_____

Education has for its object
the formation of character.

—Herbert Spencer

Your favorite famous personality is _____

The best thing that happened to you this year was _____

_____

_____

The worst thing that happened to you this year was _____

_____

_____

The funniest thing that happened to you this year was _____

_____

_____

What we did on Thanksgiving. _____

_____

What we did at Christmas. _____

_____

What you did during the summer. _____

_____

_____

Books you read this year. _____

_____

_____

_____

This year you learned how to _____

_____

_____

Your chores were _____

_____

_____

You must do the thing you think you cannot do.

—Eleanor Roosevelt

SCORE ONE FOR OUR TEAM

The year was _____

Sports you participated in. _____

_____

Your team name was _____

The captain was _____

The coach was _____

Games won _____ games lost _____

Your position was _____

What you enjoyed most about each sport. ____ _____

_____

_____

What you found most challenging. _____

_____

_____

Sports moments we will never forget. _____

_____

_____

Awards you or your team received. _____

_____

photos

When the One Great Scorer comes
to write against your name,
He marks—not that you won or lost—
but how you played the game.

−Grantland Rice

BE ALL YOU CAN BE

Extracurricular activities and lessons you participated in. _____

_____

Where and when you were involved. _____

_____

Who was the instructor(s)? _____

_____

What fascinated you most about each? _____

_____

Things you did to improve your knowledge and skills in each activity. _____

_____

_____

_____

To encourage your development in these skills we _____

_____

_____

_____

Which activity brought you the most satisfaction? _____

_____

Awards, honors, and special recognition for each activity. _____

_____

_____

_____

Money cannot buy sunsets, singing birds,
and the music of the wind in the trees.

−George Horace Lorimer

GOD BE IN MY HEART

The church we attended. _____
_____

Our pastor (priest) was _____
_____

Your Sunday school teacher was _____
_____

Special friends you enjoyed. _____
_____

Programs you participated in. _____
_____
_____

Your favorite chorus or hymn. _____
_____

For family devotions this year we _____
_____
_____

Significant prayer requests this year. _____
_____
_____

God answered our prayers by _____
_____
_____

A spiritual milestone in your life this year was _____
_____
_____

A noble deed is a step toward God.

−Josiah G. Holland

Personal goals we helped you set for the year _____

1. _____
2. _____
3. _____
4. _____

This is how you want to grow personally. _____
_____
_____

This is how you want to grow spiritually. _____
_____
_____

This is how you want to improve your relationships with others.
_____
_____

These are the plans you made to reach your goals.

1. _____
2. _____
3. _____

These are the steps you took to reach your goals.

1. _____
2. _____
3. _____

The progress you made toward each of your goals for this year.

1. _____
2. _____
3. _____
4. _____

The fear of the Lord is the beginning of knowledge.
— Proverbs 1:7

FAMILY COMINGS AND GOINGS IN _____
(year)

Significant family news events. _____
_____
_____

World news events. _____
_____
_____

Intriguing guests we had in our home. _____
_____
_____

To help others in our community we _____
_____
_____

Struggles our family overcame. _____
_____
_____

Things that brought us special happiness. _____
_____
_____

The most fun thing we did was _____
_____
_____

The most interesting places we visited were _____
_____
_____

Leftovers in their less visible form are called memories.
Stored in the refrigerator of the mind
and the cupboard of the heart.

—Robert Fulghum

HIGH SCHOOL YEARS

Searching, Hoping . . . Becoming

How beautiful is youth! how bright
it gleams
With its illusions, aspirations, dreams!
Book of beginnings, story without end,
Each maid a heroine, and each man
a friend!

—Henry Wadsworth Longfellow

photos

Do all the good you can,
in all the ways you can, . . .
to all the people you can,
as long as you ever can.

—John Wesley

106

HOW FANTASTIC TO BE FOURTEEN

You wanted to celebrate by _____

_____

Friends you invited. _____

_____

Activities we planned. _____

_____

_____

Foods we served. _____

_____

Gifts you received included _____

_____

_____

The most memorable moment was _____

_____

The funniest moment was _____

_____

_____

Our birthday blessing for you. _____

_____

_____

photos

God's gifts put man's best dreams to shame.

–Elizabeth Barrett Browning

107

STRETCHING YOUR MIND IN GRADE NINE

Name and address of school. _____

_____

Your favorite school subject. _____

Your favorite teacher. _____

Your most challenging subject. _____

Your best friend. _____

Your favorite food for lunch. _____

After school you like to _____

_____

We attended your open house on _____

Our observations. _____

_____

School competitions entered and awards won. _____

_____

_____

Special school projects. _____

_____

School activities and class trips. _____

_____

The part of the school day you look forward to most. _____

_____

_____

A young mind is like gelatin.
The idea is to put in lots of
good stuff before it sets.

—American Ad Council

Your favorite singing group _____

The best thing that happened to you this year was _____

_____

_____

The worst thing that happened to you this year was _____

_____

_____

The funniest thing that happened to you this year was _____

_____

_____

What we did on Thanksgiving. _____

_____

What we did at Christmas. _____

_____

What you did during the summer. _____

_____

_____

Books you read this year. _____

_____

_____

_____

This year you learned how to _____

_____

_____

Your chores were _____

_____

_____

My son, be wise, and make my heart glad.

—Proverbs 27.11

SCORE ONE FOR OUR TEAM

The year was _____

Sports you participated in. _____
_____

Your team name was _____

The captain was _____

The coach was _____

Games won _____ games lost _____

Your position was _____

What you enjoyed most about each sport. _____
_____
_____

What you found most challenging. _____
_____
_____

Sports moments we will never forget. _____
_____
_____

Awards you or your team received. _____
_____

photos

A person without a sense of humor
is like a wagon without springs,
jolted by every pebble in the road.

—Henry Ward Beecher

BE ALL YOU CAN BE

Extracurricular activities and lessons you participated in. _____

_____

Where and when you were involved. _____

_____

Who was the instructor(s)? _____

_____

What fascinated you most about each? _____

_____

Things you did to improve your knowledge and skills in each activity. _____

_____

_____

_____

To encourage your development in these skills we _____

_____

_____

_____

Which activity brought you the most satisfaction? _____

_____

Awards, honors, and special recognition for each activity. _____

_____

_____

_____

Studying the arts establishes a basic relationship between
the individual and the cultural heritage of the human family.

−Charles Fowler

GOD BE IN MY HEART

The church we attended. _____

_____

Our pastor (priest) was _____

_____

Your Sunday school teacher was _____

_____

Special friends you enjoyed. _____

_____

Programs you participated in. _____

_____

_____

Your favorite chorus or hymn. _____

_____

For family devotions this year we _____

_____

_____

Significant prayer requests this year. _____

_____

_____

God answered our prayers by _____

_____

_____

A spiritual milestone in your life this year was _____

_____

_____

The reward for a good deed is to have done it.
—Elbert Hubbard

Personal goals we helped you set for the year _____

    1. _____

    2. _____

    3. _____

    4. _____

This is how you want to grow personally. _____

_____

_____

This is how you want to grow spiritually. _____

_____

_____

This is how you want to improve your relationships with others.

_____

_____

These are the plans you made to reach your goals.

    1. _____

    2. _____

    3. _____

These are the steps you took to reach your goals.

    1. _____

    2. _____

    3. _____

The progress you made toward each of your goals for this year.

    1. _____

    2. _____

    3. _____

    4. _____

In youth we learn; in age we understand.

—Marie Von Ebner-Eschenbach

FAMILY COMINGS AND GOINGS IN _____
(year)

Significant family news events. _____
_____
_____

World news events. _____
_____
_____

Intriguing guests we had in our home. _____
_____
_____

To help others in our community we _____
_____
_____

Struggles our family overcame. _____
_____
_____

Things that brought us special happiness. _____
_____
_____

The most fun thing we did was _____
_____

The most interesting places we visited were _____
_____
_____

*I was my father's son, tender and only beloved
in the sight of my mother.*

—Proverbs 4.3

LOOK WHO'S FIFTEEN!

You wanted to celebrate by _____

_____

Friends you invited. _____

_____

Activities we planned. _____

_____

_____

Foods we served. _____

_____

Gifts you received included _____

_____

_____

The most memorable moment was _____

_____

The funniest moment was _____

_____

_____

Our birthday blessing for you. _____

_____

_____

_____

_____

photos

Whoever is happy will make others happy too.

—Anne Frank

GOING PLACES IN GRADE TEN

Name and address of school. _____

_____

Your favorite school subject. _____

Your favorite teacher. _____

Your most challenging subject. _____

Your best friend. _____

Your favorite food for lunch. _____

After school you like to _____

_____

We attended your open house on _____

Our observations. _____

_____

School competitions entered and awards won. _____

_____

_____

Special school projects. _____

_____

School activities and class trips. _____

_____

The part of the school day you look forward to most. _____

_____

The object of all education
is to make folks fit to live.

—Laura Ingalls Wilder

What would you like to have named in your honor? _____

The best thing that happened to you this year was _____

_____

_____

The worst thing that happened to you this year was _____

_____

_____

The funniest thing that happened to you this year was _____

_____

_____

What we did on Thanksgiving. _____

_____

What we did at Christmas. _____

_____

What you did during the summer. _____

_____

_____

Books you read this year. _____

_____

_____

_____

This year you learned how to _____

_____

_____

Your chores were _____

_____

_____

Books are the most accessible and wisest of counsellors,
and the most patient of teachers.

—Charles W. Eliot

SCORE ONE FOR OUR TEAM

The year was _____

Sports you participated in. _____

_____

Your team name was _____

The captain was _____

The coach was _____

Games won _____ games lost _____

Your position was _____

What you enjoyed most about each sport. _____

_____

_____

What you found most challenging. _____

_____

_____

Sports moments we will never forget. _____

_____

_____

Awards you or your team received. _____

_____

photos

Time cannot be taken to the cleaner
and brought back as good as new.
The use of time is a very permanent thing.

—Edith Schaeffer

BE ALL YOU CAN BE

Extracurricular activities and lessons you participated in. _____

_____

Where and when you were involved. _____

_____

Who was the instructor(s)? _____

_____

What fascinated you most about each? _____

_____

Things you did to improve your knowledge and skills in each activity. _____

_____

_____

_____

To encourage your development in these skills we _____

_____

_____

_____

Which activity brought you the most satisfaction? _____

_____

_____

Awards, honors, and special recognition for each activity. _____

_____

_____

_____

Give and it shall be given unto you,
since the gifts go around and back again.

—Robert Fulghum

GOD BE IN MY HEART

The church we attended. _____

_____

Our pastor (priest) was_____

_____

Your Sunday school teacher was _____

Special friends you enjoyed. _____

_____

Programs you participated in. _____

_____

_____

Your favorite chorus or hymn. _____

For family devotions this year we _____

_____

_____

Significant prayer requests this year. _____

_____

_____

God answered our prayers by _____

_____

_____

A spiritual milestone in your life this year was _____

_____

_____

Love is the seed that always produces a bumper crop.

—Ron Pulscher

Personal goals we helped you set for the year _____

    1. _____
    2. _____
    3. _____
    4. _____

This is how you want to grow personally. _____
_____
_____

This is how you want to grow spiritually. _____
_____
_____

This is how you want to improve your relationships with others.
_____
_____

These are the plans you made to reach your goals.

    1. _____
    2. _____
    3. _____

These are the steps you took to reach your goals.

    1. _____
    2. _____
    3. _____

The progress you made toward each of your goals for this year.

    1. _____
    2. _____
    3. _____
    4. _____

The highest wisdom is kindness.
—Jewish Proverb

FAMILY COMINGS AND GOINGS IN _____
(year)

Significant family news events. _____

_____

_____

World news events. _____

_____

_____

Intriguing guests we had in our home. _____

_____

_____

To help others in our community we _____

_____

_____

Struggles our family overcame. _____

_____

_____

Things that brought us special happiness. _____

_____

_____

The most fun thing we did was _____

_____

_____

The most interesting places we visited were _____

_____

Be present at our table, Lord,
Be here and everywhere adored.

—Edgar A. Guest

THE SIMPLE JOYS OF GROWING UP

The first major project you made yourself. _____
_____
_____
_____

Your first date. _____
_____
_____
_____

Your first (boy) girlfriend. _____
_____
_____
_____

How you learned to drive. _____
_____
_____
_____

Your first car. _____
_____
_____

Your first job. _____
_____
_____

If we could sell our experiences for what they cost us,
we'd be millionaires.

—Abigail Van Buren

photos

If a task is once begun
Never leave it till it's done.
Be the labor great or small,
Do it well or not at all.

—Anonymous

124

SUDDENLY YOU'RE SIXTEEN!

You wanted to celebrate by _____
_____

Friends you invited. _____
_____

Activities we planned. _____
_____
_____

Foods we served. _____
_____
_____

Gifts you received included _____
_____
_____

The most memorable moment was _____
_____

The funniest moment was _____
_____
_____

Our birthday blessing for you. _____
_____
_____
_____

photos

You grow up the day you have your first real laugh at yourself.
—Ethel Barrymore

MEETING OF MINDS IN GRADE ELEVEN

Name and address of school. _____
_____

Your favorite school subject. _____
_____

Your favorite teacher. _____
_____

Your most challenging subject. _____

Your best friend. _____

Your favorite food for lunch. _____

After school you like to _____
_____

We attended your open house on _____

Our observations. _____
_____
_____

School competitions entered and awards won. _____
_____
_____
_____

Special school projects. _____
_____

School activities and class trips. _____
_____

The part of the school day you look forward to most. _____
_____

A master can tell you what he expects of you.
A teacher, though, awakens your own expectations.

–Patricia Neal

This is how you write your name _____

The best thing that happened to you this year was _____
_____
_____

The worst thing that happened to you this year was _____
_____
_____

The funniest thing that happened to you this year was _____
_____
_____

What we did on Thanksgiving. _____
_____

What we did at Christmas. _____
_____

What you did during the summer. _____
_____

Books you read this year. _____
_____
_____

This year you learned how to _____
_____
_____

Your chores were _____
_____
_____

To look for the best and see the beautiful
is the way to get the best out of life each day.

—Lincoln Steffens

SCORE ONE FOR OUR TEAM

The year was _____

Sports you participated in. _____

_____

Your team name was _____

The captain was _____

The coach was _____

Games won _____ games lost _____

Your position was _____

What you enjoyed most about each sport. _____

_____

_____

What you found most challenging. _____

_____

_____

Sports moments we will never forget. _____

_____

_____

Awards you or your team received. _____

_____

photos

I find the great thing in this world
is not so much where we stand
as in what direction we are moving.

—Oliver Wendell Holmes

BE ALL YOU CAN BE

Extracurricular activities and lessons you participated in _____
_____

Where and when you were involved. _____
_____

Who was the instructor(s)? _____
_____

What fascinated you most about each? _____
_____

Things you did to improve your knowledge and skills in each activity. _____
_____
_____
_____

To encourage your development in these skills we _____
_____
_____

Which activity brought you the most satisfaction? _____
_____

Awards, honors, and special recognition for each activity. _____
_____
_____

Success is failure turned inside out—
The silver tint of the clouds of doubt.

—Anonymous

GOD BE IN MY HEART

The church we attended. _____

_____

Our pastor (priest) was _____

_____

Your Sunday school teacher was _____

_____

Special friends you enjoyed. _____

_____

Programs you participated in. _____

_____

_____

Your favorite chorus or hymn. _____

_____

For family devotions this year we _____

_____

_____

Significant prayer requests this year. _____

_____

_____

God answered our prayers by _____

_____

_____

_____

A spiritual milestone in your life this year was ____

_____

_____

_____

Prayers should be the key of the day
and the lock of the night.

—English Proverb

Personal goals we helped you set for the year _____

    1. _____

    2. _____

    3. _____

    4. _____

This is how you want to grow personally. _____

_____

_____

This is how you want to grow spiritually. _____

_____

_____

This is how you want to improve your relationships with others.

_____

_____

These are the plans you made to reach your goals.

    1. _____

    2. _____

    3. _____

These are the steps you took to reach your goals.

    1. _____

    2. _____

    3. _____

The progress you made toward each of your goals for this year.

    1. _____

    2. _____

    3. _____

    4. _____

He started to sing as he tackled the thing that couldn't be done, and he did it.
—Edgar A. Guest

FAMILY COMINGS AND GOINGS IN _____
(year)

Significant family news events. _____

_____

_____

World news events. _____

_____

_____

Intriguing guests we had in our home. _____

_____

_____

To help others in our community we _____

_____

_____

Struggles our family overcame. _____

_____

_____

Things that brought us special happiness. _____

_____

_____

The most fun thing we did was _____

_____

_____

The most interesting places we visited were _____

_____

_____

"A kind word will govern me
when all the king's horses and
all the king's men couldn't."

—Jo in "Little Women," Louisa May Alcott

SO, YOU ARE SUPER SEVENTEEN!

You wanted to celebrate by _____

_____

Friends you invited. _____

_____

Activities we planned. _____

_____

_____

Foods we served. _____

_____

Gifts you received included _____

_____

_____

The most memorable moment was _____

_____

The funniest moment was _____

_____

Our birthday blessing for you. _____

_____

_____

_____

photos

My life is a tapestry woven from the threads of many beautiful lives.

– Waldemar Agow

THE KNACK OF KNOWLEDGE IN GRADE TWELVE

Name and address of school. _____
_____

Your favorite school subject. _____

Your favorite teacher. _____

Your most challenging subject. _____

Your best friend. _____

Your favorite food for lunch. _____

After school you like to _____
_____

We attended your open house on _____

Our observations. _____
_____

School competitions entered and awards won. _____
_____
_____

Special school projects. _____
_____
_____

School activities and class trips. _____
_____
_____

The part of the school day you look forward to most. _____
_____
_____

If we write but one book in life,
let it be our autobiography.

−Richard Paul Evans

What one word would you use to describe yourself? _____

The best thing that happened to you this year was _____

_____

_____

The worst thing that happened to you this year was _____

_____

_____

The funniest thing that happened to you this year was _____

_____

_____

What we did on Thanksgiving. _____

_____

What we did at Christmas. _____

_____

What you did during the summer. _____

_____

_____

Books you read this year. _____

_____

_____

This year you learned how to _____

_____

_____

Your chores were _____

_____

_____

Youth today is in search of selflessness,
and when it finds it, is prepared to embrace it.

—Mother Teresa

SCORE ONE FOR OUR TEAM

The year was _____

Sports you participated in. _____

_____

Your team name was _____

The captain was _____

The coach was _____

Games won _____ games lost _____

Your position was _____

What you enjoyed most about each sport. _____

_____

_____

What you found most challenging. _____

_____

_____

Sports moments we will never forget. _____

_____

_____

Awards you or your team received. _____

_____

photos

Every right implies a responsibility;
every opportunity an obligation,
every possession a duty.

−John D. Rockefeller, Jr.

BE ALL YOU CAN BE

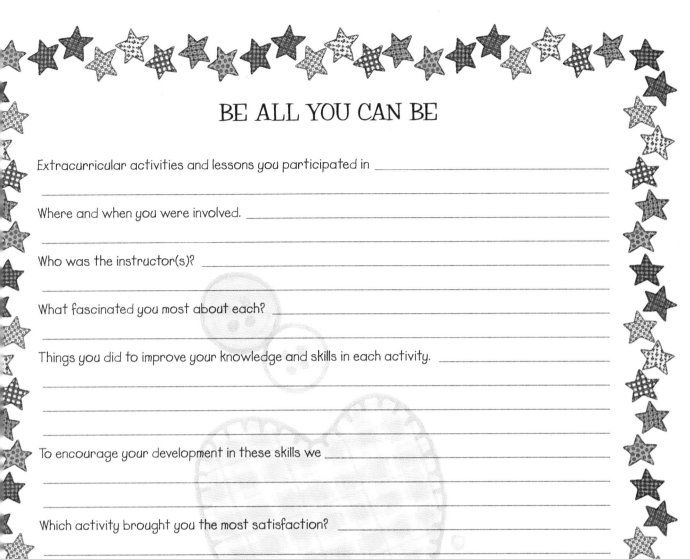

Extracurricular activities and lessons you participated in _____
_____

Where and when you were involved. _____
_____

Who was the instructor(s)? _____
_____

What fascinated you most about each? _____
_____

Things you did to improve your knowledge and skills in each activity. _____
_____
_____
_____
_____

To encourage your development in these skills we _____
_____
_____

Which activity brought you the most satisfaction? _____
_____

Awards, honors, and special recognition for each activity. _____
_____
_____

To have a good friend is the purest of all God's gifts,
for it is a love that has no exchange of payment.

—Frances Farmer

GOD BE IN MY HEART

The church we attended. _____

_____

Our pastor (priest) was _____

_____

Your Sunday school teacher was _____

_____

Special friends you enjoyed. _____

_____

Programs you participated in. _____

_____

_____

Your favorite chorus or hymn. _____

_____

For family devotions this year we _____

_____

_____

Significant prayer requests this year. _____

_____

_____

God answered our prayers by _____

_____

_____

A spiritual milestone in your life this year was _____

_____

_____

To reach the port of heaven,
we must sail sometimes with the wind
and sometimes against it;
but we must sail and not drift or lie at anchor.

—Oliver Wendell Holmes

Personal goals we helped you set for the year _____

    1. _____

    2. _____

    3. _____

    4. _____

This is how you want to grow personally. _____
_____
_____

This is how you want to grow spiritually. _____
_____
_____

This is how you want to improve your relationships with others.
_____
_____

These are the plans you made to reach your goals.

    1. _____

    2. _____

    3. _____

These are the steps you took to reach your goals.

    1. _____

    2. _____

    3. _____

The progress you made toward each of your goals for this year.

    1. _____

    2. _____

    3. _____

    4. _____

My son, attend unto my wisdom, and bow thine ear to my understanding.
—Proverbs 5:1

FAMILY COMINGS AND GOINGS IN _____
(year)

Significant family news events. _____
_____
_____

World news events. _____
_____
_____

Intriguing guests we had in our home. _____
_____
_____

To help others in our community we _____
_____
_____

Struggles our family overcame. _____
_____
_____

Things that brought us special happiness. _____
_____
_____

The most fun thing we did was _____
_____
_____

The most interesting places we visited were _____
_____
_____

A little Consideration, a little Thought for Others, makes all the difference.

Winnie-the-Pooh

GRADUATION CELEBRATIONS

Dates of senior trip. _____ Where you went. _____

What you enjoyed most _____

_____

The funniest thing that happened. _____

_____

Date of prom or senior banquet. _____ Location. _____

Your date or escort. _____

Other friends who went with you. _____

What you wore. _____

What you enjoyed most. _____

_____

The most unforgettable moment of the evening. _____

_____

Date of baccalaureat. _____ Location. _____

Baccalaureat speaker. _____

Date of graduation. _____ Location. _____

Commencement speaker. _____

Special honors and awards you received. _____

_____

_____

Your plans after graduation. _____

_____

_____

Your thoughts upon graduating. _____

_____

_____

Stand at the crossroads and look; ask for the ancient paths.

—Jeremiah 6:16

photos

Arf! Arf!

May the road rise up
to meet you,

May the wind be always
at your back

May the sun shine warm
upon your face,

The rain fall softly on
your fields;

And until we meet again,

May God hold you in
the palm of his hand.

—Traditional Irish
Prayer

YOUR FAMILY
Loving Hearts and Happy Eyes

Home is where children learn what is right,
what is good, and what is kind.

—Madame Ernestine
Schumann-Heink

photos

Kinfolks! It is such a homey
sounding word and strong, too, and sweet.

—Laura Ingalls Wilder

OUR FAMILY IS SPECIAL

Our family country(ies) of origin. _____

The languages we speak. _____

We are citizens of _____

Location of family cemetery plot. _____

Precious family heirlooms. _____

_____

Famous people in our family. _____

_____

Our family motto. _____

_____

_____

_____

Family traditions we celebrate. _____

_____

_____

_____

_____

What these traditions mean to us. _____

_____

_____

_____

_____

Family relatives who have most strongly influenced your life. _____

_____

_____

_____

_____

Traditions unite our memories of the past
with our hope for the future.

−Emyl Jenkins

YOUR FRUITFUL FAMILY TREE

GREAT GRANDFATHER

GREAT GRANDMOTHER

GREAT GRANDFATHER

GREAT GRANDMOTHER

GREAT GRANDFATHER

GREAT GRANDMOTHER

GREAT GRANDFATHER

GREAT GRANDMOTHER

GRANDFATHER

GRANDMOTHER

GRANDFATHER

GRANDMOTHER

AUNT / UNCLE

AUNT / UNCLE

AUNT / UNCLE

AUNT / UNCLE

COUSIN

COUSIN

COUSIN

COUSIN

COUSIN

COUSIN

COUSIN

COUSIN

FATHER

MOTHER

BROTHER / SISTER

YOU

BROTHER / SISTER

Memories sew us together—
years being the needle, love the thread.
—Paula Mangin

FAMILY REUNIONS

When _____

Where _____

Who was there. _____

_____

_____

The most memorable moments. _____

_____

_____

When _____

Where _____

Who was there. _____

_____

_____

The most memorable moments. _____

_____

_____

When _____

Where _____

Who was there. _____

_____

_____

The most memorable moments. _____

_____

_____

Tell your children of it,
and let your children tell their children,
and their children another generation.

−Joel 1.3

FAVORITE FAMILY RECIPES

Recipe for _____

Who created the recipe _____
Ingredients _____
_____
_____
_____

Directions _____
_____
_____
_____
_____
_____

Recipe for _____

Who created the recipe _____
Ingredients _____
_____
_____
_____

Directions _____
_____
_____
_____
_____

Meatloaf is something you eat at home.
—Robert Fulghum

HOME SWEET HOME

Your first home was located at _____

It looked like _____

We lived there for _____

Our neighbors were _____

Your first bedroom was _____

Our most cherished memory about that home. _____

_____

Other places we have lived.

Where _____   _____   _____

_____   _____   _____

How long _____   _____   _____

_____   _____   _____

Neighbors_____   _____   _____

_____   _____   _____

Your friends_____   _____   _____

_____   _____   _____

Your bedroom _____   _____   _____

_____   _____   _____

What was most unforgettable about each place we lived. _____

_____

_____

_____

_____

_____

A man travels the world over in search of what he needs and returns home to find it.
–George Moore

FAVORITE FAMILY STORIES

CHILDHOOD PRAYERS

Celebrate this child...
this angel of my dreams come true.

—Walter Dean Myers

Lord, teach a little child to pray
And then accept my prayer,
Thou hearest all the words I say
For thou art everywhere.

—Jane Taylor (1783-1824)

Lord Jesus Christ, be with me today
And help me in all I think, and do, and say

—Traditional

Be present at our table, Lord,
Be here and everywhere adored,
These creatures bless and grant that we
May feast in Paradise with Thee.

—Edgar A. Guest

For this new morning with its light,
Father, we thank Thee,
For rest and shelter of the night,
Father, we thank Thee.
For health and food, for love and friends,
For everything Thy goodness sends,
Father in heaven, we thank Thee.

—Ralph Waldo Emerson (1803-1882)

Make me, dear Lord, polite and kind
To every one, I pray.
And may I ask you how you find
Yourself, dear Lord, today?

—John Bannister Tabb

Thank you for the world so sweet
Thank you for the food we eat.
Thank you for the birds that sing.
Thank you, God, for everything!

—R. Rutter Leatham (1870-1933)

God be in my head,
And in my understanding;
God be in mine eyes,
And in my looking;
God be in my mouth,
And in my speaking;
God be in my heart,
And in my thinking;
God be at mine end,
And at my departing.

—Old English Prayer

Our Father hears us when we pray
A whisper can He hear.
He knows not only what we say
But what we wish and fear.

—John Barton (1803-1877)

Peace be to this house
And to all who dwell in it.
Peace be to them that enter
And to them that depart.

—Anonymous

Now the day is over
Night is drawing nigh,
Shadows of the evening
Steal across the sky.
Jesus, give the weary
Calm and sweet repose;
With thy tenderest blessing
May our eyelids close.

—Sabine Baring-Gould (1834-1924)

Goodnight! Goodnight!
Far flies the light.
But still God's love
Shall shine above,
making all bright.
Goodnight! Goodnight!

—Victor Hugo (1802-1885)

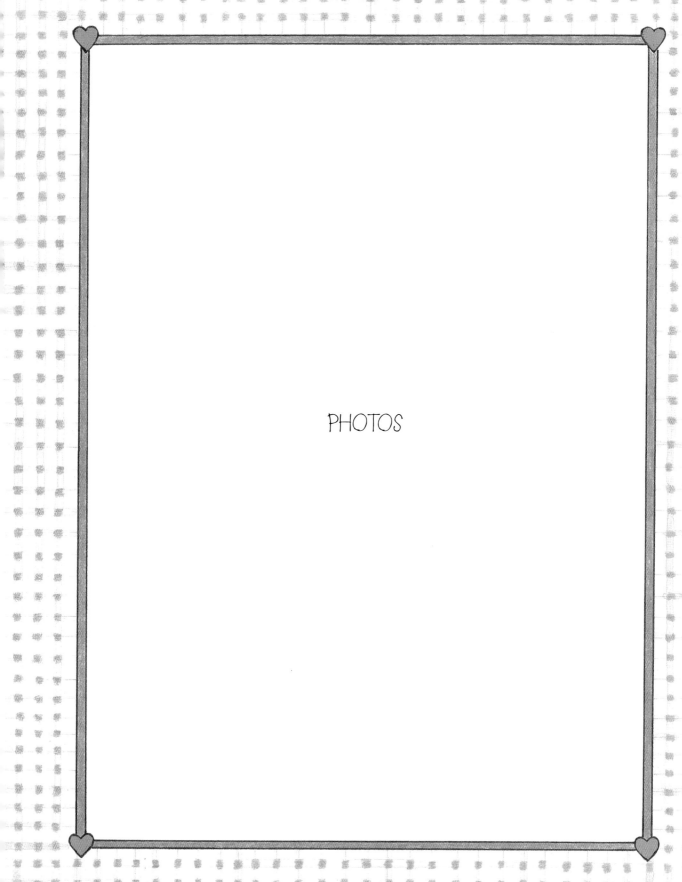

PHOTOS

PHOTOS

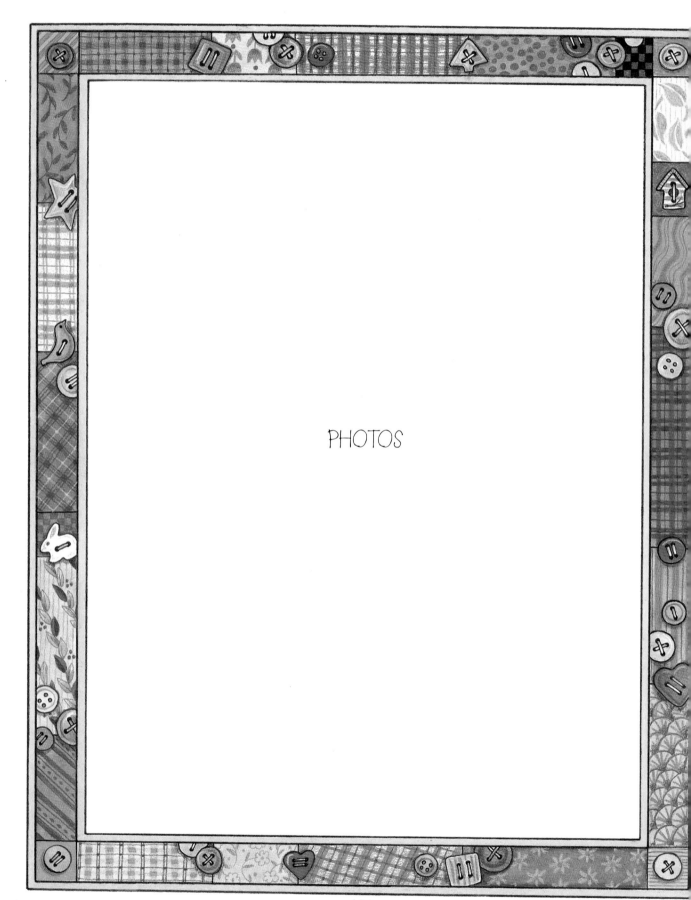

PHOTOS

PHOTOS

PHOTOS

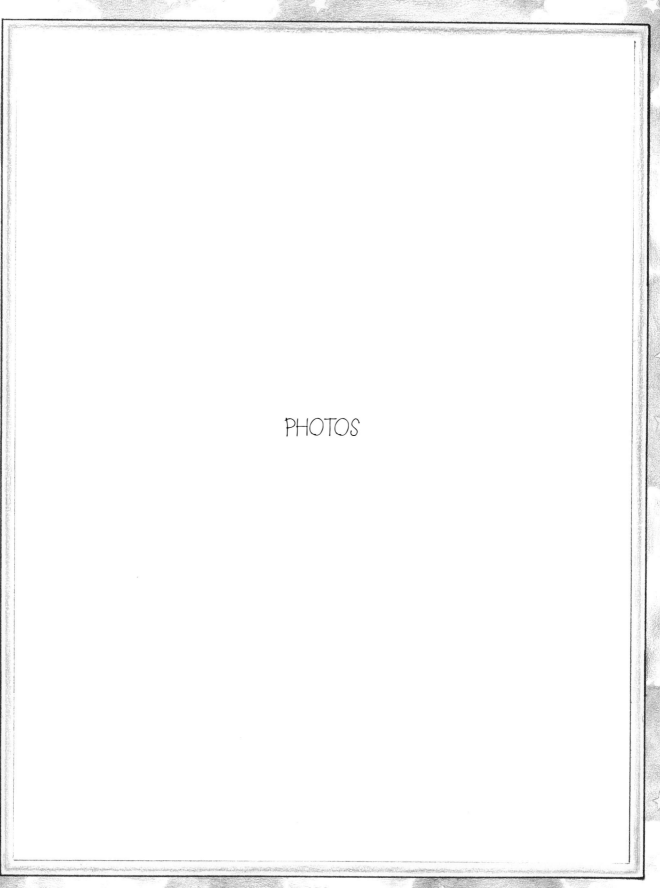

PHOTOS